P9-DTQ-614

contents

Beef Stroganoff

Makes 4 servings

PREP TIME
10 minutes

COOK TIME
25 minutes

1 tablespoon vegetable oil

1 boneless beef sirloin steak *or* beef top round steak, ¾-inch thick (about 1 pound), cut into thin strips

1 medium onion, chopped (about ½ cup)

1 can (10¾ ounces) Campbell's® Condensed Cream of Mushroom Soup (Regular, 98% Fat Free *or* Healthy Request®)

½ teaspoon paprika

⅓ cup sour cream *or* plain yogurt

4 cups whole wheat *or* regular egg noodles, cooked and drained

Chopped fresh parsley

1. Heat the oil in a 12-inch nonstick skillet over medium-high heat. Add the beef and cook until well browned, stirring often. Remove the beef from the skillet. Pour off any fat.

2. Reduce the heat to medium. Add the onion to the skillet and cook until it's tender.

3. Stir the soup and paprika in the skillet and heat to a boil. Stir in the sour cream. Return the beef to the skillet and cook until the beef is cooked through. Serve the beef mixture over the noodles. Sprinkle with the parsley.

Quick Chicken & Vegetable Stir-Fry

Makes 4 servings

PREP TIME
15 minutes

COOK TIME
15 minutes

2 tablespoons cornstarch

1¾ cups Swanson® Chicken Stock

1 tablespoon soy sauce

1 tablespoon vegetable oil

4 cups cut-up vegetables*

2 cloves garlic, minced

1 can (12.5 ounces)** Swanson® Premium White Chunk Chicken Breast in Water, drained

4 cups hot cooked rice

*Use a combination of broccoli flowerets, sliced carrots **and** green **or** red pepper strips.*

***Or 3 cans (4.5 ounces each).*

1. Stir the cornstarch, stock and soy sauce in a small bowl until the mixture is smooth.

2. Heat the oil in a 10-inch skillet over medium-high heat. Add the vegetables and cook until they're tender-crisp. Add the garlic and cook for 1 minute.

3. Stir the cornstarch mixture in the skillet. Reduce the heat to medium. Cook and stir until the mixture boils and thickens. Stir in the chicken and cook until the mixture is heated through. Serve the chicken mixture over the rice.

Chicken Tetrazzini

Makes 4 servings

PREP TIME
20 minutes

COOK TIME
5 minutes

1 can (10¾ ounces) Campbell's® Condensed Cream of Mushroom Soup (Regular *or* 98% Fat Free)

¾ cup water

½ cup grated Parmesan cheese

2 tablespoons chopped fresh parsley *or* 2 teaspoons dried parsley flakes

¼ cup chopped red pepper *or* pimiento (optional)

½ package (8 ounces) spaghetti, cooked and drained

2 cans (4.5 ounces *each*) Swanson® Premium White Chunk Chicken Breast in Water, drained

Heat the soup, water, cheese, parsley, pepper, if desired, spaghetti and chicken in a 2-quart saucepan over medium heat until the mixture is hot and bubbling.

Crusted Tilapia Florentine

Makes 4 servings

PREP TIME
10 minutes

COOK TIME
15 minutes

1 egg

2 teaspoons water

1 cup Italian-seasoned dry bread crumbs

4 fresh tilapia fillets (about 4 ounces *each*)

2 tablespoons olive oil

2⅔ cups Prego® Traditional Italian Sauce

2 cups frozen chopped spinach

   Hot cooked noodles

1. Beat the egg and water with a fork in a shallow dish. Place the bread crumbs on a plate. Dip the fish in the egg mixture, then coat with the bread crumbs.

2. Heat the oil in a 12-inch skillet over medium-high heat. Add the fish and cook for 8 minutes, turning once or until the fish flakes easily when tested with a fork. Remove the fish and keep warm.

3. Stir the Italian sauce and spinach into the skillet. Heat to a boil. Reduce the heat to medium. Cook for 2 minutes or until the spinach is wilted. Serve the sauce over the fish. Serve with the noodles.

Dripping Roast Beef Sandwiches with Melted Provolone

Makes 4 servings

PREP TIME
5 minutes

COOK TIME
5 minutes

BAKE TIME
3 minutes

1 can (10½ ounces) Campbell's® Condensed French Onion Soup

1 tablespoon reduced-sodium Worcestershire sauce

¾ pound thinly sliced deli roast beef

4 Pepperidge Farm® Classic Soft Hoagie Rolls with Sesame Seeds

4 slices deli provolone cheese, cut in half

¼ cup drained hot *or* mild pickled banana pepper rings

Kitchen Tip

You may substitute ½ of a **11.25-ounce** **package** *Pepperidge Farm® Texas Toast* **(4 slices),** *prepared according to package directions, for the rolls in this recipe. Serve the sandwiches open-faced.*

1. Heat the oven to 400°F.

2. Heat the soup and Worcestershire in a 2-quart saucepan over medium-high heat to a boil. Add the beef and heat through, stirring occasionally.

3. Divide the beef evenly among the rolls. Top the beef with the cheese slices and place the sandwiches onto a baking sheet.

4. Bake for 3 minutes or until the sandwiches are toasted and the cheese is melted. Spoon the soup mixture onto the sandwiches. Top **each** sandwich with **1 tablespoon** pepper rings.

Broccoli & Garlic Penne Pasta

Makes 4 servings

PREP TIME
20 minutes

COOK TIME
10 minutes

1 cup Swanson® Chicken Broth (Regular, Natural Goodness® *or* Certified Organic)

½ teaspoon dried basil leaves, crushed

⅛ teaspoon ground black pepper

2 cloves garlic, minced

3 cups broccoli flowerets

4½ cups penne pasta, cooked and drained

1 tablespoon lemon juice

2 tablespoons grated Parmesan cheese

1. Heat the broth, basil, black pepper, garlic and broccoli in a 10-inch skillet over medium heat to a boil. Reduce the heat to low. Cover and cook until the broccoli is tender-crisp.

2. Add the pasta and lemon juice and toss to coat. Sprinkle the pasta mixture with the cheese.

15-Minute Chicken & Rice Dinner

Makes 4 servings

PREP TIME
5 minutes

COOK TIME
15 minutes

1 tablespoon vegetable oil

4 skinless, boneless chicken breast halves (about 1 pound)

1 can (10¾ ounces) Campbell's® Condensed Cream of Chicken Soup (Regular *or* 98% Fat Free)

1½ cups water

¼ teaspoon paprika

¼ teaspoon ground black pepper

2 cups *uncooked* instant white rice*

2 cups frozen vegetable combination (broccoli, cauliflower, carrots)

*For a creamier dish, decrease the rice to 1½ cups.

Kitchen **Tip**

This recipe is also delicious using Campbell's® Condensed Cream of Mushroom Soup instead of the Cream of Chicken.

1. Heat the oil in a 10-inch skillet over medium-high heat. Add the chicken and cook for 10 minutes or until well browned on both sides. Remove the chicken from the skillet.

2. Stir the soup, water, paprika and black pepper in the skillet and heat to a boil. Stir in the rice and vegetables. Reduce the heat to low. Return the chicken to the skillet. Sprinkle the chicken with additional paprika and black pepper. Cover and cook for 5 minutes or until the chicken is cooked through.

Burgundy Beef

Makes 4 servings

PREP TIME
10 minutes

COOK TIME
25 minutes

1 tablespoon butter

1 pound boneless beef sirloin steak, ¾-inch thick, cut into 1-inch pieces

1 can (10½ ounces) Campbell's® Mushroom Gravy

1½ cups frozen whole baby carrots

½ cup frozen whole small white onions

¼ cup tomato paste

¼ cup Burgundy wine **or** other dry red wine

⅛ teaspoon garlic powder

4 cups hot cooked egg noodles

Chopped fresh parsley

Kitchen **Tip**

For Mushroom Beef, use **1 tablespoon** *Worcestershire sauce instead of the wine.*

1. Heat the butter in a 12-inch skillet over medium-high heat. Add the beef and cook until it's well browned, stirring often. Pour off any fat.

2. Stir the gravy, carrots, onions, tomato paste, wine and garlic powder in the skillet and heat to a boil. Reduce the heat to low. Cover and cook for 10 minutes or until the beef is cooked through. Serve the beef mixture over the noodles. Sprinkle with the parsley.

Ham & Pasta Skillet

Makes 4 servings

PREP TIME
15 minutes

COOK TIME
15 minutes

1 can (10¾ ounces) Campbell's® Condensed Broccoli Cheese Soup (Regular *or* 98% Fat Free)

1 cup milk

1 tablespoon spicy brown mustard

2 cups broccoli flowerets *or* 1 package (10 ounces) frozen broccoli cuts, thawed

1½ cups cooked ham, cut into strips

2¼ cups medium shell-shaped pasta, cooked and drained

1. Heat the soup, milk, mustard and broccoli in a 10-inch skillet over medium-high heat to a boil. Reduce the heat to low. Cook for 5 minutes or until the broccoli is tender.

2. Stir the ham and pasta in the skillet and cook until the mixture is hot and bubbling.

Rosemary Chicken & Mushroom Pasta

Makes 6 servings

PREP TIME
10 minutes

COOK TIME
20 minutes

2 tablespoons olive *or* vegetable oil

1½ pounds skinless, boneless chicken breast halves, cut into strips

4 cups sliced mushrooms (about 12 ounces)

1 tablespoon minced garlic

1 tablespoon chopped fresh rosemary leaves *or* 1 teaspoon dried rosemary leaves

1 can (14½ ounces) Campbell's® Chicken Gravy

1 package (16 ounces) linguine *or* spaghetti, cooked and drained

Shredded Parmesan cheese

Kitchen **Tip**

For a rustic twist, try whole wheat pasta in the recipe.

1. Heat the oil in a 12-inch skillet over medium-high heat. Add the chicken and mushrooms in 2 batches and cook until the chicken is well browned, stirring often. Remove the chicken mixture from the skillet.

2. Reduce the heat to low. Stir the garlic and rosemary in the skillet and cook for 1 minute. Stir the gravy in the skillet and heat to a boil.

3. Return the chicken and mushrooms to the skillet. Cover and cook for 5 minutes or until the chicken is cooked through. Place the pasta in a large serving bowl. Pour the chicken mixture over the pasta. Toss to coat. Serve with the cheese.

Braised Chicken with Savory White Beans & Spinach

Makes 6 servings

PREP TIME
10 minutes

COOK TIME
20 minutes

6 skinless, boneless chicken breast halves (about 1½ pounds)

⅛ teaspoon ground black pepper

½ teaspoon dried oregano leaves *or* dried basil leaves, crushed

1 teaspoon olive oil

2 cups Prego® Heart Smart Onion and Garlic Italian Sauce

1 cup white kidney beans (cannellini), rinsed and drained

1 package (10 ounces) fresh baby spinach

1. Season the chicken with the black pepper and oregano.

2. Heat the oil in a 12-inch nonstick skillet over medium-high heat. Add the chicken and cook for 10 minutes or until it's well browned on both sides.

3. Stir the Italian sauce in the skillet and heat to a boil. Reduce the heat to low. Cover and cook for 5 minutes.

4. Uncover the skillet. Stir in the beans and spinach and cook for 5 minutes or until the chicken is cooked through.

Quick Chicken & Noodles

Makes 4 servings

PREP TIME
5 minutes

COOK TIME
25 minutes

4 skinless, boneless chicken breast halves (about 1 pound)

½ teaspoon garlic powder

⅛ teaspoon paprika

1¾ cups Swanson® Chicken Stock

½ teaspoon dried basil leaves, crushed

¼ teaspoon ground black pepper

2 cups frozen vegetable combination (broccoli, cauliflower, carrots)

2 cups *uncooked* medium egg noodles

1. Season the chicken with the garlic powder and paprika. Cook the chicken in a 12-inch nonstick skillet over medium-high heat until it's well browned on both sides.

2. Add the stock, basil, black pepper and vegetables to the skillet and heat to a boil. Stir in the noodles. Reduce the heat to low. Cover and cook for 10 minutes or until the chicken is cooked through and the noodles are tender.

Quick & Easy Chicken, Broccoli & Brown Rice

Makes 4 servings

PREP TIME
5 minutes

COOK TIME
20 minutes

1 tablespoon vegetable oil

4 skinless, boneless chicken breast halves (about 1 pound)

1 can (10¾ ounces) Campbell's® Condensed Cream of Chicken Soup (Regular, 98% Fat Free *or* Healthy Request®)

1½ cups water

¼ teaspoon paprika

¼ teaspoon ground black pepper

1½ cups *uncooked* instant brown rice*

2 cups fresh *or* frozen broccoli flowerets

*Cooking times vary. To ensure best results, use instant whole grain brown rice.

1. Heat the oil in a 10-inch skillet over medium-high heat. Add the chicken and cook for 10 minutes or until well browned on both sides. Remove the chicken from the skillet.

2. Stir the soup, water, paprika and black pepper in the skillet and heat to a boil.

3. Stir the rice and broccoli in the skillet. Reduce the heat to low. Return the chicken to the skillet. Sprinkle the chicken with additional paprika and black pepper. Cover and cook for 5 minutes or until the chicken is cooked through and the rice is tender.

Beef Teriyaki

Makes 4 servings

PREP TIME
10 minutes

COOK TIME
15 minutes

2 tablespoons cornstarch

1¾ cups Swanson® Beef Stock

2 tablespoons soy sauce

1 tablespoon packed brown sugar

½ teaspoon garlic powder

1 boneless beef sirloin steak

4 cups fresh *or* frozen broccoli flowerets

   Hot cooked rice

Kitchen Tip

To make slicing easier, freeze the beef for 1 hour before slicing.

1. Stir the cornstarch, stock, soy sauce, brown sugar and garlic powder in a small bowl until the mixture is smooth.

2. Stir-fry the beef in a 10-inch nonstick skillet over medium-high heat until it's well browned, stirring often. Pour off any fat.

3. Add the broccoli to the skillet and cook for 1 minute. Stir in the cornstarch mixture. Cook and stir until the mixture boils and thickens. Serve the beef mixture over the rice.